10/7/22

My Father's World

JEFF ROGERS PHOTOGRAPHY, INC.

In memory of Jimmy Fields

This book was created without any commercial endorsements, supplies or support.
Deo est Gloria!

© Jeff Rogers, 2017

Photography by Jeff Rogers | Design and production: Sumo Design | Photo editing: Jeff Hancock

All rights reserved. No part of this work covered by the copyrights may be reproduced
or used in any form or by any means without the prior written permission of the publisher.

The copyright on each photograph in this book belongs to the photographer, and no reproductions of the photographic images contained herein may
be made without the express permission of the photographer. For information about fine art prints, contact the photographer at www.JeffRogers.com.

Library of Congress Control Number: 2017946115
ISBN-10: 0-9772400-4-5
ISBN-13: 978-0-9772400-4-3
Printed in South Korea

Scripture quotations marked NLT are taken from the *Holy Bible*, New Living Translation, copyright © 1996, 2004, 2007 by Tyndale House Foundation. Used by permission of Tyndale House Publishers, Inc., Carol Stream, Illinois 60188. All rights reserved.

The *Holy Bible*, New International Version®, NIV® Copyright © 1973, 1978, 1984, 2011 by Biblica, Inc.® Used by permission. All rights reserved worldwide.

"In Christ Alone" words and music by Keith Getty & Stuart Townsend © 2001 Kingsway Thankyou Music

"How Great Thou Art" © 1949, 1953, The Stuart Hine Trust, USA print rights admin. Hope Publishing Company. All other USA rights admin. by CapitolCMGPublishing.com

"How Firm A Foundation" by R. Keene (1797)

Jeff Rogers Photography, Inc.
www.JeffRogers.com | jeff@JeffRogers.com
P.O. Box 368 | Lexington, Kentucky 40588-0368

Then God said, *"Let there be light,"* and there was light.
And God saw that the light was good.

GENESIS 1:3 NLT

IN THE BEGINNING
God created the heavens and the earth.

The earth was formless and empty,
and darkness covered the deep waters.

And the Spirit of GOD
was hovering over the
surface of the waters.

GENESIS 1:1,2 NLT

I look up to the mountains — does my help come from there?
My help comes from the Lord, who made heaven and earth!

Have you never heard?
   Have you never understood?

The Lord is the everlasting God, the Creator of all the earth.
   He never grows weak or weary.
   No one can measure the depths of his understanding.

He gives power to the weak and strength to the powerless.
   Even youths will become weak and tired,
   and young men will fall in exhaustion.

But those who trust in the Lord will find new strength.
   They will soar high on wings like eagles.
   They will run and not grow weary.
   They will walk and not faint.

ISAIAH 40:28-31 NLT

The Lord's home reaches up to the heavens, while its foundation is on the earth.

*He draws up water from the oceans
and pours it down as rain on the land.*

The Lord is his name! AMOS 9:6 NLT

The Lord merely spoke,
    and the heavens were created.

He breathed the word, and all the stars were born.

He assigned the sea its boundaries
    and locked the oceans in vast reservoirs.

PSALM 33:6,7 NLT

Come, let us worship and bow down.
Let us kneel before the Lord our maker, for he is our God.
We are the people he watches over, the flock under his care.

PSALM 95:6,7 NLT

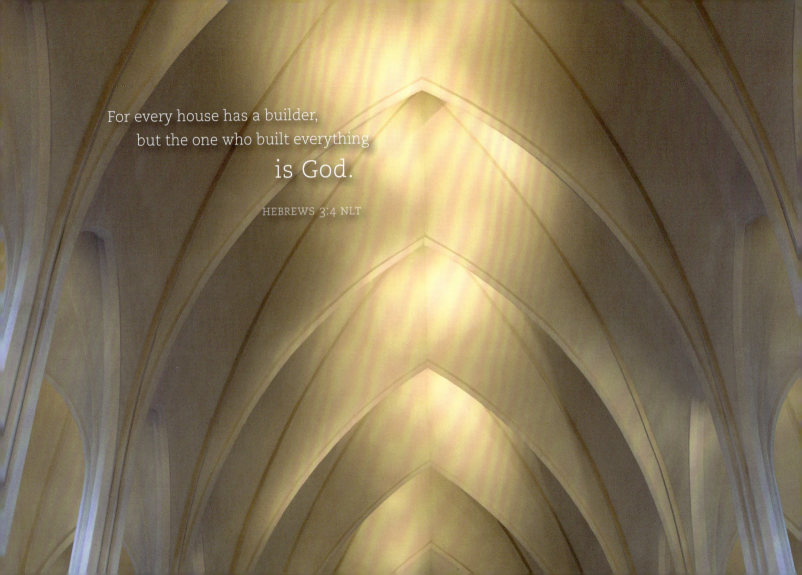

The Spirit of the Sovereign Lord is upon me,
for the Lord has anointed me
   to bring good news to the poor.

He has sent me to comfort the brokenhearted
and to proclaim that captives will be released
   and prisoners will be freed.

He has sent me to tell those who mourn
that the time of the Lord's favor has come,
   and with it, the day of God's anger against their enemies.

To all who mourn in Israel,
he will give a crown of beauty for ashes,

a joyous blessing instead of mourning,
festive praise instead of despair.

ISAIAH 61:1-3 NLT

For ever since the world was created,
people have seen the earth and sky.

   Through everything God made,
     they can clearly see his invisible qualities —
     his eternal power and divine nature.

So they have no excuse for not knowing God.

          ROMANS 1:20 NLT

The Lord is my shepherd; I have all that I need.

He lets me rest in green meadows;
he leads me beside peaceful streams.

He renews my strength.
He guides me along right paths,
bringing honor to his name.

Even when I walk through the darkest valley,
I will not be afraid, for you are close beside me.
Your rod and your staff protect and comfort me.

You prepare a feast for me in the presence of my enemies.
You honor me by anointing my head with oil.
My cup overflows with blessings.

Surely your goodness and unfailing love
will pursue me all the days of my life,

and I will live in the house of the Lord forever.

PSALM 23 NLT

Therefore, since we are surrounded
by such a huge crowd of witnesses to the life of faith,

let us strip off every weight that slows us down,
especially the sin that so easily trips us up.

> *And let us run with endurance the race God has set before us.*

Hebrews 12:1 NLT

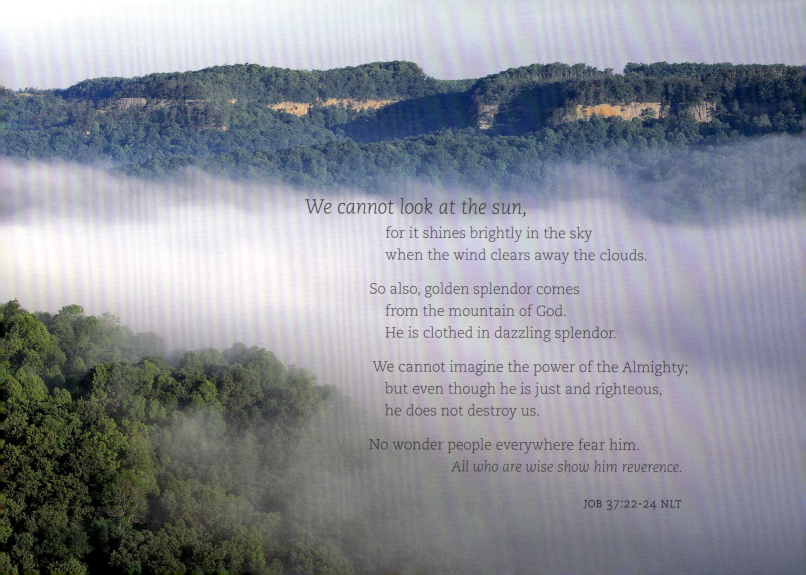

We cannot look at the sun,
        for it shines brightly in the sky
        when the wind clears away the clouds.

So also, golden splendor comes
        from the mountain of God.
        He is clothed in dazzling splendor.

We cannot imagine the power of the Almighty;
        but even though he is just and righteous,
        he does not destroy us.

No wonder people everywhere fear him.
        All who are wise show him reverence.

JOB 37:22-24 NLT

And we know that God

causes everything to work together
    for the good of those who love God
and are called according to his purpose for them.

ROMANS 8:38 NLT

The boundary lines have
fallen for me in pleasant places;
    surely I have a delightful inheritance.

PSALM 16:6 NIV

When through the deep waters I call thee to go,
The rivers of sorrow shall not overflow;

For I will be with thee thy trouble to bless,
And sanctify to thee thy deepest distress.

"HOW FIRM A FOUNDATION"
HYMN BY R. KEENE (1787)

God is our refuge and strength,
   always ready to help in times of trouble.

So we will not fear when earthquakes come
and the mountains crumble into the sea.

Let the oceans roar and foam.
Let the mountains tremble as the waters surge!

PSALM 46:1-3 NLT

Don't worry about anything;
instead, pray about everything.

Tell God what you need,
and thank him for all he has done.

Then you will experience God's peace,
 which exceeds anything we can understand.

His peace will guard your hearts and minds
as you live in Christ Jesus.   PHILIPPIANS 4:6, 7 NLT

*I am leaving you with a gift –
peace of mind and heart.*

And the peace I give is
a gift the world cannot give.
So don't be troubled or afraid.

JOHN 14:27 NLT

You will keep in perfect peace
all who trust in you,
all whose thoughts are fixed on you!

ISAIAH 26:3 NLT

*Come to me, all of you who are
weary and carry heavy burdens,
 and I will give you rest.*

Take my yoke upon you.
Let me teach you, because I am humble
and gentle at heart,
and you will find rest for your souls.

For my yoke is easy to bear, and the burden I give you is light.

MATTHEW 11:28-30 NLT

O Lord my God,

    When I in awesome wonder,
        Consider all the worlds Thy Hands have made;
    I see the stars, I hear the rolling thunder,
        Thy power throughout the universe displayed.

    When through the woods, and forest glades I wander,
        And hear the birds sing sweetly in the trees.
    When I look down, from lofty mountain grandeur
        And see the brook, and feel the gentle breeze.

    When Christ shall come, with shout of acclamation,
        And take me home, what joy shall fill my heart.
    Then I shall bow, in humble adoration,
        And then proclaim: "My God, how great Thou art!"

        Then sings my soul, My Saviour God, to Thee,
        How great Thou art, How great Thou art.
        Then sings my soul, My Saviour God, to Thee,
        How great Thou art, How great Thou art!

                "HOW GREAT THOU ART"
                HYMN BY CARL BOBERG (1865)

So we fix our eyes not on what is seen,
but on what is unseen,

since what is seen is temporary,
but what is unseen is eternal.

II CORINTHIANS 4:18 NIV

May your glorious name be praised!
May it be exalted above all blessing and praise!

You alone are the Lord.
You made the skies and the heavens and all the stars.

You made the earth and the seas and everything in them.
You preserve them all, and the angels of heaven worship you.

NEHEMIAH 9:5B,6 NLT

Don't let your hearts be troubled.

Trust in God, and trust also in me.

There is more than enough room in my Father's home.
If this were not so, would I have told you
 that I am going to prepare a place for you?

JOHN 14:2 NLT

His brilliant splendor fills the heavens,
 and the earth is filled with his praise.

His coming is as brilliant as the sunrise.
 Rays of light flash from his hands,
 where his awesome power is hidden.

HABAKKUK 3:3,4 NLT

In Christ alone my hope is found,

He is my light, my strength, my song;
this Cornerstone, this solid Ground,
firm through the fiercest drought and storm.

What heights of love, what depths of peace,
when fears are stilled, when strivings cease!

My Comforter, my All in All,
here in the love of Christ I stand.

"IN CHRIST ALONE"
HYMN BY KEITH GETTY AND STUART TOWNEND (2001)

How precious are your thoughts about me, O God.
They cannot be numbered!
I can't even count them;

they outnumber the grains of sand!

PSALMS 139:17,18 NLT

And now, dear brothers and sisters, one final thing.

*Fix your thoughts on what is true,
    and honorable, and right,
        and pure, and lovely, and admirable.*

Think about things that are excellent and worthy of praise.

PHILIPPIANS 4:8 NLT

PHOTO LOCATIONS

front cover .... Sunset near Scottish Highlands, Scotland

3 .... Sunset, Madison County, Kentucky
4 .... Sunset over Lake Powell, Arizona
6 .... Sunrise at Parinacota and Pomerape, Sajama National Park, Bolivia
8 .... Clouds, Arizona
9 .... Sunset at the Grand Canyon, Arizona
10 .... Bryce Canyon, Utah
12 .... Sunrise, Pringvellir National Park, Iceland
15 .... Sunset near Scottish Highlands, Scotland
16 .... Hallgrimskirkja Lutheran Church, Reykjavik, Iceland
17 .... Sunset and storm, Myrdalshreppur, Iceland
18 .... Glory cloud over Lake Titicaca, Bolivia
20 .... Hill and clouds, Eastern Kentucky
22-25 .... Florals, Sarasota, Florida
26 .... Vine and Branches, Kentucky
29 .... Jordan Pond, Acadia National Park, Maine
30 .... Coastal church, Hvalfjaroarsveit, Scotland
32 .... Fog and sunrise at Double Arch, Red River Gorge, Kentucky
34 .... Rainbow, Floahreppur, Iceland
35 .... Icelandic horses with rainbow, Snaefellsnes Peninsula, Iceland
36 .... Ancient church interior, Scotland

38	Portal Dolmen, Ireland
41	Rushing water, Bolivia
42, 43	Mammoth Hot Springs, Yellowstone National Park, Wyoming
44, 45	Antelope Slot Canyon, Arizona
47	Driftwood Beach, Jekyll Island, Georgia
48	Sunrise and fog, Chicago Morton Arboretum, Illinois
50	Early fall, Chicago Morton Arboretum, Illinois
52, 53	California Mission Church, California
54	Devil's Jump canoe trip, Big South Fork, Kentucky
57	Vineyard, Loire River Valley, France
58	Svartifoss waterfall, Vatnajokull National Park, Iceland
60, 61	Jokulsarlon Glacier Lagoon, Vatnajokull National Park, Iceland
62	Pawley's Island storm, South Carolina
65	Sunrise at Mirror Lake, Lake Matheson, New Zealand
66	Cross in the spring, Kentucky
68	Castle on a hill, Wales
70, 71	Aurora Borealis, Skaftarhreppur, Iceland
73	Abandoned boat, Scottish Highlands, Scotland
74	Sunrise, Pawley's Island, South Carolina
76	Cliffs of Moher, County Claire, Ireland
back cover	Sunrise at Pawley's Island, South Carolina

"We need to find God,
  but we cannot find him in noise or in excitement.

 See how nature, the trees, the flowers, the grass grow in deep silence.
  See how the stars, the moon, and the sun all move in silence."

Mother Teresa of Calcutta

"God writes the gospel not in the Bible alone,
  but on trees and flowers and clouds and stars."

Martin Luther